DYNAMIC DISCOVERY

WORKBOOK

A PROCESS OF SELF EVALUATION

BY GEORGE BISSETT

ACKNOWLEDGEMENTS

Writing this book has provided me with both pleasure and frustration: pleasure because I had long ago written out a poorly formatted and incomplete document that I used as a guide for several of my workshops; frustration because I had trouble expressing in writing what seemed so clear in my head. And then five people entered my life and things began to happen.

The first two people are Bob and Dawn Bray, who became good friends and a sounding board for my many rants and also provided me with excellent feedback. Check out our website (www.dynamicdiscovery.ca) and you will see that Bob has excellent 'helping' skills of his own.

Then I contacted Lise Merle, who had previously done some inventive consulting work for me, and told her what I was hoping to do. She provided the layout for this book. Her contributions are gratefully appreciated.

Natasha Burkholder (http://littlebcreative.com) designed all of the graphics used throughout the book – from the cover all the way to the end.

And last, but far from least, is Christina (Chrissy) Rice who has converted the book into the various formats and has looked after publishing issues, all social media and other marketing chores: find her at www.completeadminsolutions.ca

CHECK FOR INFORMATION AT WWW.DYNAMICDISCOVERY.CA.

TABLE OF CONTENTS

OVERVIEW

This workbook is a companion piece to the book, Dynamic Discovery and is intended to help you fully incorporate that process of self-evaluation for change.

Dynamic Discovery is not about being presented with a good dose of reality or harshly being told to get on with things. It is more to do with helping individuals find better ways of meeting their needs and taking responsibility for themselves and their lives.

Counseling often involves delving into the past, whereas in Dynamic Discovery, we believe that the solution lies in the present and the future. We visit the past to a lesser extent than those who use other therapies. This is not a criticism of those who use other therapies – it is simply a way in which Dynamic Discovery is different.

In Dynamic Discovery, the past is seen as the source of our wants and of our ways of behaving. Not only are the bad things that happened to us there, but our successes are there, too. The focus of Dynamic Discovery is to learn what needs to be learned about the past, but to also move as quickly as feasible toward empowering the client to satisfy his or her needs and wants in the present and in the future. It is our present perceptions that influence our present Behavior, and so it is these perceptions that the Dynamic Discovery process helps the client to work through.

Our objectives are:

*   To show you how to create a better life for yourself – based on your self-evaluation.

*   To help you to determine whether your current actions and decisions will lead you to the goals or successes you want for yourself.

*   To help you find better ways to meet your needs.

*   To help you understand and take responsibility for the choices you make, so you are able to strengthen your relationships through personal change.

*   To help you self-evaluate symptoms and complaints and change them, to better deal with current relationship problems.

Our major premise is that we are responsible for our own choices, decisions, goals, and the general degree of happiness in our own lives. Through Dynamic Discovery, you will come to understand why and how you make the choices that determine the course of your life, recognizing that:

1.   You have freedom to make choices.

2.   You must take responsibility for your choices.

3. Your Behavior should be considered in its totality.

4. Your capacity to change is in you.

5. You are only a victim if you choose to be.

The single most important question to aid your self-evaluation is, "How is that working out for me?" From there, the Dynamic Discovery process will help you change whatever Behavior is preventing you from getting or becoming what you really want.

Throughout this workbook, you will be asked a number of questions In order to keep you focused on where you want to go, on a daily basis or longer term. Some of those questions are:

*   What do I want?

*   What is that going to do for me?

*   What's stopping me?

*   What's important to me here?

*   What's working well?

*   What can be better?

*   What resources are going to support me?

Because Dynamic Discovery is very much a therapy of hope – based on the conviction that we are products of the past, but we do not have to go on being its victims – I encourage you to adopt and adapt the strategies and activities described in the Dynamic Discovery book and in this workbook in order to allow the process to work for you.

EVERYBODY NEEDS CONTROL

We try to control ourselves, other people, and situations to meet our own needs or to get what we want.

Often we are not aware that we are doing this. We may walk to the shop to buy something we want, but be unaware of our surroundings as we walk down the street. Indeed, we may be 'a million miles away' in our minds, daydreaming about something but still ending up in the shop we wanted to go to; we were able to control our direction and our walking, even though we were not aware of what we were doing!

Everybody needs a certain amount of control to meet their needs for power, belonging, freedom and fun. The most important word to notice here is 'everybody'.

You need a certain amount of control. Your partner needs a certain amount of control. The boss needs a certain amount of control, but so does the worker. The parent needs a certain amount of control, but so does the child. The customer needs a certain amount of control, but so does the shopkeeper.

When people fail to recognize that the other person also has a need for control, the stage is set for conflict. If, however, we are willing to negotiate and compromise, we can find ways to co-operate and create a better life.

dynamic discovery

Sometimes, we ask for what we want. This respects the sense of control of both parties. (If you don't believe asking is an attempt to gain some control, consider the outrage in the workhouse when Oliver Twist 'asked for more'.) Sometimes instead of asking, we demand what we want. But demanding what we want ignores the other person's sense of control, and they will want to resist us.

Control is all around you. If you're scared to go to work and stay in bed instead, you are controlling your situation, at least to the extent of not going to work. If you buy a lottery ticket, you are trying to exercise a little bit of control over your future, however poor the chances of winning. If you hear there's going to be a gasoline shortage and you hoard gasoline, you are trying to gain a little control over the future. If you boss people around, you are trying to get control over them.

And if they find a way to cheat you or con you, they are trying to get some of their control back.

What We Can Control

There are four aspects to everything we do: Thinking, Doing, Feeling and Physiology.

So if you are angry, you may: think 'What a rat such-and-such a person is' (Thinking), kick the dog (Doing), have that burning angry feeling (Feeling), and have adrenalin and other chemicals in your bloodstream (Physiology).

dynamic discovery
a process of self-evaluation

A small change is all that is necessary: A change in one part of the system can affect change in another part of the system. We then have the sense that positive changes will at least continue, and may expand and have beneficial effects in other areas of the person's life.

Of these four aspects, the one that is most in your control to change is Doing. Regardless of how you feel, you almost always have some control over what you do.

Law, morality, politeness and many other human institutions recognize this fact. You may feel angry with me, but you are not entitled to assault me; you are expected to exercise some control over what you do.

The key point to remember about changing what you do is this:

If you do something that is better than what you are doing now, there is a good chance that your thoughts and feelings will also change in a more positive direction, even if change may not come right away.

To put it more simply:

Doing something better than what you are doing now will push your feelings towards the positive.

Again:

Do better to feel better.

Don't wait until you feel good about doing something that might help. If it might help, do it even though you may not feel enthusiastic at the time.

Doing comes first.

First, do better. Then feel better.

When you notice that you are not getting what you want, you need the flexibility to change what you are doing in order to get a different result. The human nervous system can be thought of as goal-seeking, and we tend to get what we focus on, so one of the key questions is 'What do you want?'

Well-formed outcomes are an important tool for ensuring that you get more of what you want in your life. In order to identify where to focus your attention, ask yourself:

What do I currently believe is holding me back from achieving what it is that I really want to achieve?

_____

_____

_____

_____

_____

_____

_____

EXAMPLES OF DYNAMIC DISCOVERY LANGUAGE

Human essential needs can be broken into two categories. One is the need to love and be loved at all times during the course of a lifetime. The other is the need to feel worthwhile to one's self and others. In order to feel worthwhile, one must maintain a satisfactory standard of behavior. In other words, if a person is drinking to avoid facing reality, then he or she is not maintaining a satisfactory standard of behavior and not feeling worthwhile. Everyone has these essential needs, but our abilities to fulfill them vary.

The process of fulfilling the essential needs requires, first and foremost, involvement with other people who are in touch with the reality of the world. Without involvement with other people, we try to fulfill the basic needs in unhealthy ways, like overeating or abusing drugs. Not knowing how to fulfill essential needs always leads to pain, either physical or emotional, for the client or those around him or her.

Dynamic Discovery does not concern itself with a client's past. Neither do we deal with unconscious mental processes. We acknowledge distress but focus on success. You will be encouraged – through self-evaluation – to find your own solutions. Different forms of questions enable this process. In these ways, Dynamic Discovery is a very different approach to problem-solving.

Dynamic Discovery tends not to use typical psychology labels – like 'neurotic' or 'dysfunctional' – because these terms tend to stereotype people. Responsibility and irresponsibility are two terms commonly used in Dynamic Discovery:

- Responsibility refers to the ability to fulfill one's needs and to do so in a way that doesn't interfere with someone else fulfilling their needs. For example, responsible students do their own homework. Dynamic Discovery holds that we learn responsibility through involvement with another responsible person. We can learn and re-learn responsibility at any time in life.

- Irresponsible people cannot fulfill their own needs, or they fulfill their needs at the cost of negatively affecting someone else. Irresponsible students look for someone else to do their work. If a parent does the homework for the child, the parent is also being irresponsible. The student who doesn't do their homework is harming their own learning process and being a burden on those around them. The parent who does the homework is harming the student by not teaching that child responsibility.

WANTS AND CHOICES

Wants

There are people who spend all their time getting what they want and they're not happy people. So is there more to Dynamic Discovery than just getting what you want?

We actually ask, "What do you REALLY want?" rather than simply "What do you want?" Let's elaborate on this.

A man goes into a DIY shop and asks for a paintbrush. "What do you want to do?" asks the lady behind the counter. "I want to paint my car," replies the customer. "Maybe a can of spray paint is what you want," suggests the shop lady.

The moral is... if this man had received what he wanted, would he have gotten what he really wanted – which presumably was a reasonably presentable car (spray-painted) rather than a streaky one (brush-painted)?

People come to us with all sorts of problems, but these problems might be classified into three (often overlapping) situational types:

1.   My picture does not meet my needs (although it is easy enough to achieve in Behavior).

2.   I cannot make my picture happen (i.e., translate into Behavior, although it would be need-satisfying).

3.   The inner logic of my picture has problems.

An example of Situation 1 is the picture of drugs. I can get drugs easily enough, but ultimately they do not meet my needs (although I only put them into my picture album in the first place because they appear to meet them).

An example of Situation 2 is where I know that the picture of joining the local choir is need-satisfying, but I am too shy to approach the club premises. I lack the skills or knowledge to make my picture happen in the real world of Behavior.

Situation 3 is directly relevant to this discussion about wants. The paintbrush, for example, appears to be what I want, but there is a flaw in my logic, in the way I connect my pictures together. Paintbrushes are simply not for painting cars!

The way people handle (or generally mishandle) time management is full of examples of logic breakdowns.

Many people come to the Dynamic Discovery program because their lives are messing up, in spite of apparently getting what they want. In a sense, they have all the paintbrushes they have ever asked for and they wonder why they are still unhappy. In the Dynamic Discovery world, happiness is first getting what you NEED before focusing on what you want! In your daily life, you hope that what you want will ultimately get you what you need, but sometimes you get it wrong.

One important theme in Dynamic Discovery is self-evaluating the effectiveness of your current wants:

If you had what you want, would you be happy? (Yes) ___ (No) ___

Is this what you really want? (Yes) ___ (No) ___

How much do you know about what you want?

_____

_____

_____

Do you also want the consequences of what you want? (Yes) ___ (No) ___

How many years, or lifetimes, will it take you to get what you want right now?

_____

_____

_____

Follow-Up Questions

What is one task you have been putting off – a task that you fear doing – even though you know that by completing it you will free up your time and mind?

_____

_____

_____

How would completing this task improve the quality of your life?

_____

_____

_____

In actual workshops, there is a question about Dynamic Discovery that is posed in various ways by group members:

> Are the people you are referring to getting material things or things such as better relationships, marriages, peace, more time? I know many people who have all the possessions they want, but are miserable or feel a void. I also know people who have opted out of ownership to a simpler lifestyle to gain more control over their lives.

Our answer is:

> We are motivated to get what we want. We feel frustration when there is a gap between what we want and what we are getting. For as long as we are alive and kicking, there will always be that gap between what we want and what we are getting, because there is always a new want or situation. So what matters is how we

manage that gap between what we have and what we want. Some things we can move towards more effectively; some we must learn to accept less of than we would like, and some we need to take out of our wants altogether or push them way back in the queue. In many ways, Dynamic Discovery is about how we manage that frustration and what we do with it.

To say that people are motivated by what they want is not the same thing as saying that getting what they want will inevitably 'make' people happy. A lot of Dynamic Discovery is about negotiating the conflicts between your wants and those of others, or between contradictory wants you might have. Sometimes it's the way in which people go about getting what they want that makes trouble for them.

> *"Happiness is not getting what you want, but wanting what you have."*

>   -   Rabbi Hyman Schachtel

While that quote is somewhat of a twist of how we understand 'want' in Dynamic Discovery as it dircets our Bchavior, it provides a powerful insight as to how to address many of the realities of our lives.

It seems that after we secure one want, goal, etc. we are on to the next. What I may see as a desire to continually improve, others may see as perpetual dissatisfaction.

Dynamic Discovery makes a distinction between our Needs (survival, love and belonging, achievement/power/recognition, fun, and freedom) and our Wants (which are the pictures we have in our head as to how to satisfy those needs). Our wants or pictures change as to how to best fulfill our needs because we change. As a child, my picture of fun was playing ball with my friends. As an adult, my picture has changed to going to a movie or having friends over for dinner. With new information, experiences, etc. we look for different ways to satisfy our needs. Without changing wants, we remain static – with no life mission or growth. It is true that what you see as a way to improve, others may see as perpetual dissatisfaction. That's because they are looking at the world through their perception of life, with their own pictures and wants as to how to best get their needs met. Fortunately, it is not through their perception that you must live your life, but through your own.

You can move yourself towards what you want by self-evaluating how your life is currently to allow you to determine where you really want to go, and the key to getting there is to write it out in detail. Follow these steps to get you started on your journey:

1. State your goal in positive terms: What do I want?

_____

_____

_____

_____

2. Self-evaluate your goal: Am I doing this for myself or someone else?

_____

_____

_____

_____

Does my goal depend solely on me?

(Yes) ___   (No) ___

3. Define your goal: Where, when, how, and with whom do I want it?

_____

_____

_____

_____

_____

_____

_____

_____

4. Describe the details of the process:

What will I be doing to get my goal?

dynamic discovery

_____

_____

_____

_____

_____

_____

How will I know I'm achieving it?

_____

_____

_____

_____

What will I see, hear, and feel when I have it?

_____

_____

_____

_____

5. Identify the resources you need.

What resources do I have now?

_____

_____

_____

_____

What resources do I need to acquire?

_____

_____

_____

_____

Have I ever achieved this goal – or something like it – before?

_____

_____

_____

_____

What happens if I act 'as if' I already have it?

_____

_____

_____

_____

6. Is your goal ecological – that is, without direct sexual competition? (Yes) __ (No) __

What is the real purpose behind why I want this goal?

_____

_____

_____

_____

What will I lose or gain if I have it?

_____

_____

_____

_____

What will and won't happen if I get it?

_____

_____

_____

_____

What will and won't happen if I don't get it?

_____

_____

_____

_____

7. Describe the first step you will take toward achieving your goal.

_____

_____

If you are struggling with one or more or all of the above, there is a way to clarify. You may have never really thought about what you want or what you might be capable of, because you may be so focused on your daily routine that you just haven't taken the time to think about your own future. Suppose somebody said you could have anything you wanted in the world – anything at all – how would you know what to choose? What would you do if you knew you could not fail? Write out your answer:

_____

_____

_____

_____

_____

Think about what would happen if you actually succeeded at Doing whatever you wrote above. Most people doing this exercise find that they start off with some conventional answer almost automatically – but when they have had some time to actually absorb the idea of being unable to fail, they come up with an entirely different, and sometimes surprising, answer. Your answer will tell you what you really want to achieve.

Write out your answer to:

'What would happen if you succeeded?'

_____

_____

_____

Choices

Choice is not totally avoidable. We cannot choose not to choose! It has been noted many times by many behavioral professionals that doing nothing is still a choice – and that is only one of the realities that we deal with in Dynamic Discovery. The inevitability of choice is not a limitation. It is within our power to make some change in our own lives. The following notes suggest a structure for learning to deal with the unavoidable choice. Needless to say, they should not be followed in a cookbook fashion.

What is the problem? Although it sometimes takes a lot of time, there is a critical point in Dynamic Discovery when you will become aware of how your life differs from your ideal world; how what you have is not the same as what you want. The more specific this awareness, the better. This process requires that the problem area be identified already.

What are the OPTIONS open to you? To answer that question, you can ask yourself:

- What do I want?

- What is that going to do for me?

- What's stopping me?

- What's important to me here?

_____

- What's working well?

_____

- What can be better?

_____

- What resources are going to support me?

_____

The above questions may help you identify one or more approaches to dealing with the problem. Depending on the seriousness and complexity of the problem, it may be necessary to extend the list of options by consulting outside experts.

However, you should always ensure that one option describes a 'no change' scenario. This is the 'zero option'. It can also be helpful to include possibilities that appear far-fetched or even funny.

Establish the INEVITABILITY OF CHOICE. Sometimes it can be useful to get you thinking of choice by remarking to yourself, "When I leave here, I can choose to leave things as they are. I can choose the 'no change' angle or I can opt for one of the other plans.

I cannot foresee the future, but good planning depends heavily on good anticipation. That's the best I can do."

Answer the following questions:

1. Is it possible not to choose? (Yes) ___ (No) ___

2. What do I think of having a closer look at each of the options before I choose?

_____

_____

_____

3. What are the possible CONSEQUENCES of each of these options? Here, you question each option on your list:

4. What do I think might happen if I chose this option?

_____

_____

_____

_____

_____

5. If I choose this, what else am I probably choosing?

_____

_____

_____
_____
_____

6. How might I feel once I make this choice?

_____
_____
_____
_____
_____

7. What would be good about it for me and what would be bad about it?

_____
_____
_____
_____
_____

8. How certain can I be about these outcomes?

_____
_____
_____
_____

How do you EVALUATE each of these options, bearing in mind their consequences? If you could award a satisfaction rating to each of these options where the maximum score is 100%, what would you give to each option? This will help you compare the options and make an evaluation of each.

Which CHOICE will you take? Maybe all your scores are between 90% and 100%, but even if they are between 10% and 15%, you still have a choice and you can pick whichever seems best or whichever is least bad. You may think you have no choice when none of the available choices score well. Writing down the different options and giving each a score can help you see that, no matter how bad they may be, some choices are better than others.

How can you PLAN to make that choice a successful reality? This has to do with planning and rehearsing. Look at plans for carrying out this choice. Do you need to learn new skills? Why not practice them now?

Making the best choices to satisfy your needs applies in any environment, no matter how restrictive or impoverished.

All choices occur within boundaries. If you're in a city and you want to go out tonight, you have a myriad of choices. The boundaries to those choices will include legal restrictions, financial restrictions, other people's rules and so on, but essentially you have hundreds, if not thousands, of choices. If you're living in a refugee camp, the boundaries are much tighter. If you're locked in a room, they are tighter still. So while you will almost always have choices, they occur within boundaries.

Sometimes these boundaries are such that all the choices are painful. A child in an orphanage who's locked into the boiler room for the night has choices (curl up, bang on the door, try to sleep, etc.) but they are terribly constricted by the boundaries imposed by whoever used their power to throw them in there. They are also painful choices. People often have to choose between painful alternatives because that's all that is available. There is also the question of 'choices' which are made so fast that we are not aware of making them.

Choices are part of everyday life, no matter what situation we are in.

Our approach is to say something like "we understand that in the past you may have been a victim and you may feel like a victim now, but you can choose to see this placement at the group home as punishment or an opportunity to stop your mind from bouncing, and assess where you are and move ahead. You can choose to run away (explore consequences here – more restrictive placement, jail) or you can choose to accept some of the help that is available – school, job counseling, activities that may get you to your community or home faster."

Finally, look at your Behavior. Is your Behavior getting you closer to home or further away?

dynamic discovery

Attitude And Empowerment

The longer I live, the more I realize the impact of attitude on life. Attitude, to me, is more important than facts. It is more important than the past, than education, than money, than circumstances, than failures, than successes, than what other people think or say or do. It is more important than appearance, giftedness or skill. It will make or break an organization or a home.

The remarkable thing is you have a choice every day regarding the attitude you will embrace for that day. You cannot change your past, and you cannot change the fact that people will act a certain way. You cannot change the inevitable. The only thing you can do is to play on the one string you have, and that is your attitude.

I am convinced that life is 10% what happens to us and 90% how we react to it. And so it is with you – we are in charge of our attitudes.

In Dynamic Discovery, the emphasis on choices (in attitudes and actions) is empowering, and can be very liberating – but we need to realize that the available choices can be restricted by other people, the weather, etc.

You have choices about how you feel in a given situation, and that how we feel will often be most easily influenced by the control you take over your Total Behavior – particularly your actions and thoughts.

Sometimes you may choose to feel sad because feeling sad is an appropriate response for you to your life circumstances at a particular time; e.g. when that circumstance is sad and the response is to grieve. How you choose to behave in terms of your actions and thoughts will govern how you may gradually come to resolve a difficult issue for yourself. For example, if you were grieving or otherwise choosing to feel sad or depressed, you could choose to drink alcohol, take drugs, sleep all day, isolate yourself from others, think that life is not worthwhile or that you have a bad 'lot' in life, etc., etc... or you could choose to seek support from a counselor or good friend or family member, get some exercise, seek small enjoyments in life, think that you will overcome this bad period, and so on.

Where 'Attitude' comes in is that you need to take on the attitude that you are in control of your life, and that how you act and think is your easiest route to altering how you feel. Attitude should not involve just 'getting on' with things in spite of emotional pain, because people need to recognize their pain, seek assistance to help them deal with it, have it validated – at least validate it themselves – but then make positive choices to help them deal with the issues.

It's important not to confuse thinking with feeling. You have the most control over what you do, and more control over what you think than what you feel. Therein lies the power of positive thinking.

Let that sink in ...

What you think and do has total influence over how you feel.

Everything can be taken from you but one thing: The last of your human freedoms – to choose one's attitude in any given set of circumstances. Choices are always available. Conditions may make some choices less desirable and change the nature of the choice, but it's still there. If you plan a picnic and it rains on that day, you can still have your picnic, but you have to choose to have it indoors or choose to get wet. The choices are not restricted, but their impact has changed.

Your attitude is a choice, much like other choices.

For instance, an individual may be experiencing grief issues over the loss of a loved one and, out of need, he convinces himself that he has to take on an attitude of nonchalance. This may help him to deal with his grief for the moment, but not in the long run. If, however, he believes that 90% of life is about how he reacts to it, he may take on an 'attitude' of 'I can handle it'. Rather than dealing with and working through the trauma, he instead deals with it only on the surface. With counseling – if he gets counseling – he may be enlightened on how attitude is important but can be overstated, and he may come to realize that attitude is not the be-all and end-all coping tool.

With Dynamic Discovery, you will learn how to make the changes that put your problems where they belong: behind you.

Automatic choices or forgotten choices are still choices. It is important to remember that you are always responsible. You may make a routine choice and do not put much thought into it, but you are still responsible. The example of driving a car and being a million miles away in your mind is a great example. After all, if by being a million miles away you got into an accident, then you are responsible for that choice even though you did not mean to make it. That consequence may make you more aware next time.

Some of what we do is genetically encoded and in that sense, perhaps it is done at a subconscious level.

Are those 'choices' we make outside our awareness really choices at all, or are they automatic actions or forgotten choices or actions taken while we are asleep (in the sense of not being aware of what is going on)? This is important because so much of life involves routines carried out beyond our awareness (like driving a car while we are elsewhere in our minds), and when we describe these as choices, we seem to 'blame' those who carried out these actions.

Sometimes we cannot choose the development of politics, social changes, etc. that force us to be in awkward situations. But when someone is in a certain situation – such as being a refugee or an orphan, or being abused, etc. – they still have choices they can make, such as living a dignified life, submitting to the authorities, accepting the fact of not having parents, etc.

You can make choices in any immediate situation which could make a great difference to your ultimate quality of life.

Being truly present in the moment includes an immediate consciousness of every choice, which requires the highest process of reasoning and thinking.

Consider the following ...

• Everything you do or have is the result of the choices you make.

• You will always experience what you create (through your choices).

1. What is a decision you know you need to make and you have put off?

_____

_____

2. What action would you have to take in order to achieve your outcome?

_____

_____

3. What is the potential risk of taking this position?

_____

_____

4. How will it feel to have accomplished this action?

_____

_____

Empowerment

Dynamic Discovery is not about being presented with a good dose of reality or harshly being told to get on with things. It is more to do with helping you to self-evaluate in order to find better ways of meeting your needs and taking responsibility for yourself and your life.

Once the basics for survival – food, clothing and shelter – are catered to, humans have other more complex psychological needs – such as the need to love and be loved; the need to belong; the need for power, self-worth, freedom, and happiness. Each of us has these needs but some need more of one thing than another, and what makes it harder is that often you are not actually aware of exactly what it is that you need.

Dynamic Discovery is used to bring about change while respecting the needs of others. Learning to assess one's needs and to alter one's life, in small but positive ways to fulfill those needs, is a significant step towards progress and ultimately taking responsibility for one's own life.

In Dynamic Discovery, our basic human needs are classified under five headings:

- Power – which includes achievement and recognition; feeling worthwhile;

- Love and belonging – which includes groups as well as families or loved ones;

- Freedom – including independence, autonomy or your own space;

- Fun – including pleasure and enjoyment;

- Survival – nourishment, shelter and reproduction.

One of the core principles of Dynamic Discovery is that, whether we are aware of it or not, we are always acting to meet these needs, but not necessarily in an effective manner.

Socializing with people is an effective way to meet our need for belonging. Sitting in a corner and crying in the hope that people will come to us is generally an ineffective way of meeting that need – it may work, but it is painful and carries a terribly high price for ourselves and others.

If life is unsatisfactory or we are distressed or in trouble, we need to check whether we are succeeding in meeting our basic psychological needs for power, belonging, freedom and fun.

Because we're alive and functioning, the survival need is normally being met. It is in how we meet the other four psychological needs that we run into trouble.

To check out whether you are meeting your needs, the three basic questions that are asked are:

1. What do you want?

_____

_____

_____

2. What are you doing to get what you want?

_____

_____

_____

_____

3. Is it working?   (Yes) ___   (No) ___

Then it's time to make workable plans to get what you want. Consider the following:

4. If you had a magic potion that allowed you to wake up tomorrow with everything you ever wanted in your life, how would your life be different?

_____

_____

_____

_____

_____

_____

5. What would your life consist of?

_____

_____

_____

_____

Dynamic Discovery has to be about things that are in your control – things that are possible to do.

For instance, maybe you can't make your spouse talk to you, but you can talk to them; maybe you can't get your teenage son to treat you with respect, but you can decide that you will no longer provide a laundry and catering service to a son who treats you with contempt; you can't make the company give you a promotion but you can look for it, lobby for it and apply for the job when it comes up.

32

Dynamic Discovery will empower you by emphasizing the power of doing what is in your control to do. In Dynamic Discovery, changing what we do is the key approach to changing how we feel and to getting what we want.

Control is also very important. Our focus is on individual choices and sticking to what is within our own control to do, while respecting other people's rights to meet their own needs.

In Dynamic Discovery, we delve into the past but not to a great extent. The past is seen as the source of individual wants and the origins of ways of Behavior, but there are both good and bad things there. Our emphasis is on learning from the past but focusing on the present and empowering individuals to satisfy their needs and wants now and in the future.

It is very much a process of hope, based on the conviction that we are products of the past but we do not have to go on being its victims.

TOTAL BEHAVIOR AND CHANGE

As human beings, we have many needs – which can be grouped under five headings:

1. **L**ove and Belonging

2. **A**chievement, Power and Recognition

3. **F**reedom

4. **F**un (enjoyment, appreciation)

5. **S**urvival (and safety)

When our life is out of balance, we can look at these needs and assess whether one or more of them is being frustrated. If so, we can focus on things we can do – that are within our control – to bring about a better balance. These do not have to be major things. Here is a list of the major needs, and examples of how we might meet them:

Love And Belonging

Giving and receiving love and/or sex; being part of something; belonging to groups; having or being someone to talk to; receiving attention; sharing experiences; supporting teams, political parties; working; chatting; greeting.

Achievement, Power And Recognition

Visualizing what you would be doing, thinking, and feeling if your self-esteem was strong and positive; what it would look like to feel powerful, achieving, and worthwhile; to 'see' yourself as competitive, confident, and a 'winner'.

Freedom

Space; spreading my wings; elbow room; time to myself; independence; autonomy.

Fun

Enjoyment; pleasure; appreciation; laughter; games, learning.

Survival

Food; clothing; shelter; health.

If life is unsatisfactory, if we're distressed or in trouble, a quick check of whether we're meeting our four basic LAFF needs (the fifth, Survival, is implied)is in order, because it's often in an attempt to meet those needs that we run into trouble.

Checking In With Yourself To Stay On Track

Whether we are aware of it or not, we are all the time acting to meet our LAFF needs. But we don't necessarily act effectively.

So, in order to keep on track to where you want to get, use the following checklist of questions to ask yourself:

1. What do I want?

_____

2. What is that going to do for me?

_____

3. What's stopping me?

_____

4. What's important to me here?

_____

5. What's working well?

_____

6. What can be better?

_____

7. What resources are going to support me?

_____

The Key Is What We Want

Nobody ever gets up in the morning and says, "I must meet my Love and Belonging need today." We are more likely to say something along the lines of, "I wonder if Mary is free for lunch today" or "Maybe we can get the gang together on Friday night." We want to have lunch with Mary or to marry John or to go out with our pals on Friday night or we want 'our' football team or 'our' political party to win.

So what really drives us as social beings is our wants. We don't think of our needs as such. We think of what we want, behave to get what we want, fantasize about what we want and so on.

As well, asking yourself (and others) questions with the appropriate structure and voice tone can help change your state and focus.

Define Your Question

Instead of asking yourself "Why am I lazy?", ask yourself "How can I change my state so that I become energetic?" If your brain does not come up with an immediate answer, then ask with intensity and expectation and you will eventually advance in that direction.

Differences

There are many ways to meet your needs. We can think of the things we want as ways of meeting our needs – effectively or ineffectively.

We all need to eat, but I want a steak and you want a pizza. Not only do our wants often differ, but the details of our wants are very specific. I want a sirloin steak, cooked medium, in a black pepper sauce; you want a deep-filled ham and mushroom pizza with no peppers. I want a socialist government that will pay for social services for people on low incomes; you want a capitalist government that will cut welfare and taxes. To the extent that we can respect the fact that other people – including those nearest and dearest to us – want different things than we want, we can live in harmony. If we cannot respect these differences, then we must live in conflict.

To get what we want, we behave. We are engaging in one Behavior or another from the time we are born to the time we die. But this Behavior has components, and when these are put together, we can think of them as constituting Total Behavior.

Total Behavior

At any time, four things are happening for you: what you are doing, what you are thinking, what you are feeling, and what is going on in your body.

Sometimes these activities work in harmony. For instance, if you are pleased, you may be smiling (doing), thinking positive thoughts, feeling content, and physically relaxed. If you are angry, you may be shouting (doing), thinking angry thoughts, feeling that you are in a rage, have your heart beating quickly and your muscles tensed up.

Often, the four activities are going in different directions. If you are sitting in a dentist's waiting room and you hear the drill starting up, your feelings may tell you to run but your thinking may tell you to stay. Your body may be tensed up with heart racing and adrenaline pumping. And you may be idly thumbing through an out-of-date copy of Hello! magazine.

You could say that at any one time, we are behaving in each of these four ways: feeling, thinking, doing, physiology. We can call this combination our Total Behavior. If we can change one of these behaviors, then we have a good chance of changing the others.

A small change is all that is necessary. A change in one part of your system can affect change in another part of your system, and you may have the sense that positive changes will at least continue and may expand and have beneficial effects in other areas of your life.

It is hard to change our feelings directly. It is easier to change what we are thinking, and easiest of all to change what we are doing.

So the golden rule is: if you want to change how you feel, begin by changing what you are doing or what you are thinking. Easy to say and hard to do? Yes! Let's look at it a little more closely.

Changing How You Feel

Consider the four components of Behavior: Doing, Thinking, Feeling, Physiology. Which do you focus on moment-to-moment?

You always know how you feel, but if feelings are your moment-to-moment guide to what to do next, you may be in difficulty; if you feel angry, you may lash out at someone or you may become depressed to suppress the anger.

Moreover, if there is something you need to do, you may make the mistake of waiting until you feel right about it before you do it. Suppose there's an important phone call you have to make but which you never actually 'feel' like making when the time comes to do it. If you are led – on a moment-to-moment basis – by how you feel, there is a good chance you will never make the call or that you will postpone it until you are in trouble and cannot put it off any longer.

But you can change your focus so that you are purpose-led instead of feelings-led. You are still very aware of your feelings – they are the warm, beating heart of your life – but your purpose is your moment-to-moment guide and your orientation is towards doing.

So now you make your telephone call, even though you don't feel like making it at this particular moment. With the phone call made, you – hopefully – feel relief, a return of energy – perhaps even a little elation.

Paradoxically, by focusing on what you can do rather than on what you feel, you arrive at a point where your feelings become pleasant and positive.

Another example: if you feel tired and tense and stressed and you go for a brisk, 10-minute walk – even though you don't feel like it – you are likely to have more energy and to be in a better mood afterwards. Here you have done something (gone for a walk) which has changed your physiology (increased energy), and now you feel better.

Sometimes the good feeling takes longer to arrive. If you are grieving over the end of a relationship or over a death, you will – hopefully – get to the point where you are doing things you want to do – seeing friends, taking a break and so on – but it may be a long time before this 'feels' right and before you start to feel good. But you will get there, if you have the courage to keep working at it – and it will help greatly if you have friends to help you along the way.

This raises an important point about the things you want. Sometimes you cannot move ahead unless you change what you want.

Suppose you want the renewal of a relationship more than anything else, but you know it simply isn't going to happen. For a time, part of the pain you feel comes from wanting something you can never have or can never have again. This wanting and this pain is part of grieving. In time, you must come to wanting somebody or something else in place of what you have lost. If you persist in wanting the person you have lost, you must be prepared to reduce the importance of that want to you – you must allow other wants to take priority.

Here are five questions (and statements) to help expedite your self-evaluation process:

1. What have I been doing to solve my problem(s)?

Begin by looking at what you have been doing to solve the problem

_____

_____

_____

_____

_____

2. How is what I'm doing helping me get what I want?

It might be helpful to think about your behavior to see how each method is working for you.

_____

_____

_____

_____

3. What might be some other things I could try?

You could look at some new ideas to try when you are ready to look at moving toward a plan for meaningful change

_____

_____

_____

_____

4. Which idea would I like to try first?

You can identify several possibilities. Write out what you think about trying any of them

_____

_____

_____

_____

_____

_____

_____

5. When?

Figure out when to talk about whether your plan is working.

_____

_____

_____

6. Then ask, "What is in it for me? What is in my best interest?"

_____

_____

_____

_____

This approach is geared toward taking the steps needed to put you on track to finding better ways to meet your needs. Just as the essence of life is building loving relationships and a solid career or other meaningful activities that contribute to society, the essence of Dynamic Discovery is building and maintaining relationships and improving home, social and work performance to meet one's basic needs.

So in order to bring about change in your life, you must do something different or change what you want. If you want to be a good athlete but you spend your mornings in bed, you must change what you do – get up and start running instead of snoozing – or change what you want – perhaps decide that what you really want out of life is to be a couch potato.

Notice that doing something different involves a change in thinking. Instead of thinking, "I must have this," you decide (and making the decision is also a form of thinking) that "I will settle for that."

Define Your Questions

Instead of asking yourself "Why am I lazy?" ask yourself "How can I change my state so that I become energetic?" If your brain does not come up with an immediate answer, then ask with intensity and expectation – and you will eventually advance in that direction.

Your thoughts are somewhat under your control. They wander off on their own every few minutes (if not every few seconds!), but you need to be willing to change what you think in order to change what you do. Sometimes, however, your emotions are so strong – with grief or depression, for instance – that all you can change is what you do, and even your thoughts have to follow afterwards.

Bear in mind that when you want what you've never had, you must do what you've never done. Change allows that to happen.

CONFLICT IN RELATIONSHIPS

The two major personality types are extroverts (also referred to as extraverts) and introverts. These are opposite ends of the spectrum of personality traits. Extroverts and introverts become friends and/or fall in love all the time – because opposites attract – but may find it difficult to build a strong relationship or marriage because of communication differences.

Though relationship conflict is inevitable, resolving conflict and improving communication is easier when you understand introverted and extroverted personality types.

There are eight personality types anchored by two temperaments – introversion and extroversion – which creates 16 personality styles. Under those two umbrellas, there are four different functions: feeling, thinking, sensing and intuition.

Noted psychologist Carl Jung believed that introverts draw energy from their inside world. They take time to observe situations and determine a viable course of action before jumping in. Extroverts, on the other hand, look to the outside world for energy. They thrive in social situations and tend to be more outspoken than their more reserved counterparts.

According to an article posted on PsychologyToday.com, these differences may in fact be hard-wired into a person's biology. In a 2009

dynamic discovery

study, PET scans were utilized to measure cerebral blood flow in both introverted and extroverted individuals. The researchers noted that there was increased activity in the frontal lobe in introverts while extroverts experienced increased blood flow to the back of the brain.

One is not better than the other, just different.

The only person any of us can change is ourselves, and we will only change if it makes sense to us and gets us something we want. For instance, an angry person will only work to learn how to cope/manage/deal with their anger when it makes sense to them. We do not willingly change for others, but we do change for our own reasons. This is because all human Behavior is deliberate and purposeful and intended to achieve something or get us something we want – whether it works or not.

Behaviors

So, why do we humans do certain things, act certain ways, when that particular Behavior seems to not work? The simple answer is memory. Nearly everything we do is dictated by memory. When we smell something, we automatically check our memory bank to determine whether the smell has been experienced before. If it has been, we have the solution to the question. If it hasn't, we then have an unanswered question. If we find the answer to that question – maybe by asking someone else – we have one more 'fact' in our memory banks. If we do not answer the question, we still have a memory of a smell that is simple unlabeled.

Whenever we meet someone, we scan our memory to determine whether we've met that person before and, if so, what they mean to us. If they are strangers, we determine who they remind us of and what that person meant to us. Based on memory, we form instant judgments. It's not about right or wrong, good or bad, strong or weak; it's all about memory. AND FEELINGS.

A person who uses arrogance or anger or snideness – to the extent that many or most people do not want to be in their company – is likely doing it because at least one time it worked, or appeared to work, for them. A memory is created such that the mind asks "What do we do when we feel like this?" and the answer is, "We act arrogant/angry/snide" and so we do – long after it quits working.

Why do you do the things you do? Because you want to. And you want to because that's what you've learned to do. And you believe you're right and anyone who disagrees with you is wrong. You have to feel that way because your perception is your reality. If you believe it to be true then it is true – for you!

The solution to any human problem is always simple, but seldom easy. Never confuse simple with easy. The solution to any addiction is to simply cease the addictive Behavior, but if it was an easy thing to do, then far more addicts would discard their addictive Behavior. Even amongst those addicts who do work at overcoming their addiction, some 85% relapse – because overcoming is NOT easy.

What is a decision you know you need to make and you have put off making?

_____

_____

_____

_____

CHOICES AND DEPRESSION

In Dynamic Discovery, depression is seen as a way of dealing with the gulf between what we have and what we want. Because depression is seen in this way, we always hold out for the possibility of overcoming depression. And, as is clear below, Dynamic Discovery does not see depression as being bad all the time. Sometimes it is better than the alternatives.

What is important is not to trap ourselves in depression. What is more important is to know that the path out of depression begins with changing what we want or changing how we behave.

Depression can do four things for us – and knowing what these are can help us to begin the climb out into the light. These four things can be thought of under the acronym ACHE.

A for Anger

Depression is often considered an alternative to anger, and sometimes it can be better to choose depression than anger. If you make a habit of lashing out when anything goes wrong, you can alienate other people and often make matters worse. Consider how many relationships anger has destroyed. Consider how many lives anger has destroyed. Anger has its place, and it often gives us the energy for change, or the energy to stand up for ourselves. But it can be destructive, too. Depression

dynamic discovery

can be a safe, temporary alternative to anger. It becomes unsafe when it goes on for too long or we use it too readily.

C for Control

Depression gives us a certain amount of control over people and situations. It may help us to avoid taking risks, to stay in a safe environment. To a certain extent, people will try to avoid upsetting us when we are depressed. If we are absolutely devastated by something that has happened, depression may give us the only control over our lives that we can handle at the time. The price for this control, of course, is very high – because of the suffering that comes with depression. By definition, nobody enjoys depression – if we did, it would not be depression.

H for Help

Depression brings us a certain amount of help. This may be help from friends, from a doctor or from an institution. Some people need this help for a time. Again, if it goes on too long, people may stop helping us and, in any event, depression is a high price to pay for the help we get. But why don't we just ask for help? For many of us, it isn't such an easy thing to do, to say "I am in a bad way; please help me." Many of us have the tendency, when asked "What's wrong?" to reply, "Nothing," – even though there may be a great deal wrong. Depression can get us help without us having to ask for it.

E for Excuse

Depression can excuse us for not doing what we should do. It can be a way of avoiding pain. If I am depressed, how can I be expected to get out and about, dress well, work, face my problems, etc.? Yet, very often, it is only by doing these things – even, at an extreme, by doing something, anything at all – that I can start to climb out of a depression.

So, if I am depressed, Dynamic Discovery would say that I can begin to climb out of the depression by taking action.

I have no direct control over the feeling of depression. I may, if I am in the depths of depression, have little or no control over my thoughts. All I can control is what I do. Maybe all I can do is get out of bed and sit by the window, or get out of bed and go downstairs.

When I can do a little more, I should try to do something more. Ideally, I should focus on small things that I want and that I can get.

Maybe I want my children back living with me, but I can't get that because they've grown up and flown the nest – but maybe I can telephone or write to them. Maybe I can spend more time with my friends or more time doing something else that I want to do and that is unattainable.

I also need to change what I want – in this case, to accept that my children will never return to live with me.

Is this easy? No. Sometimes it's very difficult and takes a long time. Our feelings, thoughts and actions are linked, but sometimes we have to do something for quite a long time before our feelings follow and become positive.

Although this work can be slow (though it isn't always slow) it's worth the effort. Injunctions to "snap out of it" and to "pull yourself together" are often ineffective. If we could snap out of it, we would. The work of changing our Behavior even while our feelings remain low will be far more effective in the long run.

Medication And Depression

Many people have a great deal to say about medication, but I do not have the qualifications to discuss it, and my attitude is that I have nothing useful to contribute on the topic. But I believe that, whether you are on medication or not, Dynamic Discovery can make your life better.

Behavior

The 'Behavioral Car' is a way of illustrating a key aspect of Dynamic Discovery: imagine that our Total Behavior is like a front-wheel drive car in which the two wheels at the back represent Feeling and Physiology and the two front wheels represent Doing and Thinking. It is by changing the direction of the two front wheels that we change the direction of the car. In other words, to change how you feel, change what you do and/or what you are thinking.

Sometimes people who are attending a therapist say, "I've got depression. What are you going to do about it?" And their therapist will just as often reply, "I know what you mean. I'll get back to you on it." But they seldom do.

However, Dynamic Discovery is a most useful tool for anyone who wishes to cease depressing and choose a more positive Behavior. Unfortunately, orthodox medicine tends to most often stuff people with drugs. To be fair, they don't rule out counseling altogether, but claim that a patient with severe depression needs to have the individual's chemical imbalance corrected before they are able to benefit from counseling.

I have had occasion to meet up with people who will not – for their own reasons – take medication but wish to stop depressing. Under such circumstances, I explain the Control Car and how, through Dynamic Discovery, they might be able to deal with depression – if that's what they really want.

Orthodox medicine holds that people are depressed because of a chemical imbalance – and, to me, that is like saying a man was running because he was sweating. In each case, the chemical imbalance and the sweat are the physiological component of the Total Behaviors chosen to depress and to run.

54

All cases are, of course, different, but it is better to do something rather than nothing, and it is better to do something enjoyable rather than just 'do'. That is to say it is better to walk up and down than just sit, and it is better to go out for a walk with the dog or play tennis or whatever turns you on than just walk up and down.

The principle of tiny bites also applies. If you feel you cannot manage a long walk, how about around the back yard or to the end of the block?

Look at your problem through the following six questions:

1. What?

_____

2. Which?

_____

3. Who?

_____

4. When?

_____

5. Where?

_____

6. Why?

_____

'Why?' is the only question that doesn't ask for specific detail. The answer to 'Why?' is usually 'Because...' and a historical or theoretical explanation. You may get specific detail in response to 'Why?', but that will only be a lucky accident. In Dynamic Discovery, we seldom ask 'Why?' – instead relying on the other five questions.

Much attention has been focused on how to overcome depression, but it is often forgotten that it is not always wrong to depress. Most of us depress three or four times a day. It is often a wise choice: it is wiser than anger, which could have physical consequences. Often we need time to withdraw; bereavement is an obvious example. Depressing here and there is quite legitimate. It is only when the Behavior continues and no longer provides effective control that it needs to be addressed.

The point is that it is a choice.

IMPORTANT NOTE

The foregoing discussions about conflict and behaviors and choices make clear that we are governed by our nature (personality) and perceptions – all of which are merely reflections of our Values and Beliefs systems, which are important because:

•　　Our beliefs become our thoughts

•　　Our thoughts become our words

- Our words become our habits

- Our habits become our values

- Our values become our destiny

The 'Should' Question Exercise

Divide a sheet of paper into three columns. At the top of the first column, write the words 'I Should...'

Then in that column, write down all the things that you feel you should be doing. The list can be as long or as short as you like.

Look at your list and rearrange them into the order of 'most important'. Then beside each 'I Should...' statement, ask yourself 'Why?' and write down the answer in the second column.

Then for each 'I Should...' statement, ask yourself 'Says Who?' and write the answer in the third column.

This exercise helps you to find the basic beliefs you have about yourself. The 'Says Who?' column will challenge your assumptions and show how you have been programmed to believe certain things that are causing problems for you. For example:

<u>I Should...</u>

Find a different job

Become more aggressive

Why?

To earn more money

To take control of situations

Says Who?

My Wife

My mother

Now go through your list again, but this time rewrite all statements as 'I Could...' These will turn into your affirmations. These affirmations will target the things in your life that you may want to focus on.

For those of you who are really 'stuck' because of your 'limiting' Values and Beliefs, you will find a free downloadable workbook (What Are Your Values?) on our website (www.DynamicDiscovery.ca) that was specially devised to provide a concise, systematic way to change those Values and Beliefs that are interfering with your ability to be happy.

INTRODUCTIONS

In actual workshop (group) situations, everyone in the group is introduced the same way, through asking the key questions to elicit information about what individual group members want, and to begin evaluations of what they have been doing in order to achieve those wants. You can use the same process to work on your own wants.

If the answers do not come easily to you, please be aware that most people give little thought to what they want or what they might be capable of, because they are so focused on their daily routines that they just don't take the time to think about their own future – which is the route to a wasted life. This is your opportunity to use our process to answer the 'want' question.

Key Questions

1. What has been going on that led you to (or back to) Dynamic Discovery?

_____

_____

_____

_____

2.   What have you done to try to resolve your problems?

_____

_____

_____

_____

3.   How did it work out? Did it help you get what you want?

_____

_____

_____

_____

4.   What do you want?

_____

_____

_____

_____

5.   If you got that, what would it mean to you?

_____

_____

_____

_____

It may appear that our method of questioning ignores a lot of important information. The overall goal during the introductory session is to find out what you want and if your current and past behaviors are pertinent to moving you toward that goal. This exercise is for you to identify what you really want so that you are able to make a start at getting what you want and need – regardless of past behaviors – to find solutions to the areas of challenge for you.

The fact that you have been taking action to try and change your life is encouraging, but those actions may not help get what you really want. The problem lies not with your willingness to change or to work for change, but with your inability to find an effective means of doing so.

If your answer to Question #5 above – directly or indirectly – was that you wanted 'to be happy', then we can help you get started with that. However, if your answer was somewhat – or a whole lot – less than 'happy', then I would invite you to go back and work through all five questions again – because we have found that when clients describe the feeling or sensation they seek from getting their wants satisfied, none of them want anything less than happiness, peace, contentment and strength. Because happiness can mean a whole list of things, and it will be helpful if you develop your own list of definitions.

If you arc finding it difficult to determine what you really want, just utilize the following process which may provide an answer for you:

Suppose somebody said you could have anything you wanted in the world, anything at all, how would you know what to choose?

One way is to ask yourself "What would I do if I knew I could not fail?" and note your answer.

Think about what would happen if you actually succeeded at achieving your answer. Most people who do this exercise find that they start off with some conventional answer almost automatically, but when they have had some time to actually absorb the idea of being unable to fail, they come up with an entirely different – and sometimes surprising – answer. Your answer will tell you what you really want to achieve.

_____

_____

_____

_____

_____

_____

In a group situation, it is at this point that the group members realize they all want basically the same things, regardless of how different they may be as individuals. They are able to identify with their common wants – which is taking a positive approach.

FEELINGS

For Dynamic Discovery purposes, we want to deal with emotional feelings, not the physical aspect of feelings. Just trying to feel better doesn't work; although we try and try to change our world by trying to feel better, nothing changes.

We also deal with conscience and guilt as two separate emotions. We define conscience as the emotional hotplate which allows us to evaluate our personal interest in an issue. Conscience, upon understanding, is that feeling of deep regret. Guilt is when we don't like or want the feeling we get from an action, but we do the action anyway. Administering through guilt is difficult, because we all understand guilt differently and apply it differently.

If administering through guilt worked, we would only have to use it once to get others to change their behaviors. In the case of a child being told that their behavior causes pain to Mommy and/or Daddy, that pain is not real to them and they can't relate to it. If, however, their conscience allows them to remember the pain they felt from a behavior, then they can find value in changing that behavior.

Experiential learning has more value than theoretical learning because of the mind's ability to memorize the thoughts, feelings and actions associated with the learning.

The question to address is: 'What kinds of feelings have you been struggling with just prior to your decision to enroll in Dynamic Discovery?' At this point, you should make a list of all the feelings that you have been having problems with, both now and over the course of your life. (Do this on the lines below.) Not limiting the feelings to current feelings takes the focus away from today and removes any confessional tone to the discussion, and offers you a chance to honestly self-evaluate these feelings without fear of being criticized or judged.

_____

_____

_____

_____

_____

_____

_____

_____

_____

_____

Now name a feeling you have had sometime in your life that you did not like having. This is a feeling that did not help you get what you wanted. It may be a feeling you are struggling with right now, but it doesn't have to be.

_____

_____

_____

_____

You likely don't find it difficult to describe the past feelings that have caused you the most disruption and discomfort in your life. You can describe these feelings as "unwanted."

Key Questions

(Please note that we are only dealing with feelings at this time and you should check to see if any of your responses are thoughts instead of feelings.)

1. What feelings have you had in your life that you didn't like?

(For a list of unwanted feelings compiled from actual group sessions, see Page 132.)

_____

_____

_____

_____

_____

_____

_____

_____

2. How many hours a day are you dealing with feelings you don't like?

_____

_____

_____

_____

3. Which of the feelings on your list have you not felt?

_____

_____

_____

_____

4. Are your feelings the biggest problem you have? In other words, if you could somehow feel better, would things be 'alright'? (Yes) ___   (No) ___

5. How would you like to be feeling?

   (For a list of wanted feelings compiled from actual group sessions, see Page 132.)

_____

_____

_____

_____

It is possible for you to start feeling these emotions if you are interested.

The choice is yours. You must decide.

Your road to ongoing recovery could involve the challenge of reaching for the feelings you want to be experiencing.

Discussion Of FEAR As The Root Of Our Unwanted Feelings

In group sessions, when we write out our list of unwanted feelings, the word FEAR is listed on the board in capital letters to denote its importance in our lives. Having established how seriously these feelings have affected the lives of the group members, we move into a discussion on FEAR.

We talk of the nature of fear, with the natural 'fight or flight' response. You likely understand that fight or flight responses occur over the short term, but you may not have considered the phenomenon of living with these sensations over an entire lifetime.

In an actual group session, asking the group members to define FEAR is usually unproductive – often producing only silence – so we provide the dictionary definition: 'a distressing emotion aroused by impending danger, evil or pain'. This definition implies that FEAR is a simple response to a threat. When our needs are not getting met, we experience FEAR.

At this point, the question to the group members is, "Do you want to have FEAR?" The answer is always, "NO!" The next question is, "Do you want to be able to respond to a threat?" The answer here is always, "YES!" We don't dwell on this discussion, except to make the point that FEAR is merely a response to a threat. The threat does not have to appear real to anyone other than the person experiencing the FEAR. The point is made that it is a very smart system that perceives a threat and responds to it.

Fear is the 'driving' feeling behind all other unwanted feelings and is the root of guilt, anger, and so on. As a group, we discuss the fear that is contained in the other feelings on the list, like getting caught in the feeling of guilt. Quite often, the group likes to deny any fear in guilt, so they are asked a hypothetical question: "When you meet someone whom you like and who obviously likes you, do you ever think that this person won't like you once they get to know you?" There is usually general agreement.

What is your answer to that question?

(Yes) ___ (No) ___

In an actual workshop, we go through some of the feelings on the list that the group creates, and we talk about what fears pertain to the unwanted feelings. Anger is a feeling that can easily hide the fear factor. Very often, people who are angry in no way appear to be full of fear. However, if we accept fear as a simple response to a threat, we can see the fear in an angry person. Many people who use anger as a continuous controlling Behavior are simply

68

using a purposeful and selective Behavior for trying to meet their needs.

Using the consistent questioning approach, the connection to fear is made in each and every instance. This moment in the session is often a turning point for the group members.

If you're struggling with a fear, you can use a visualization exercise to test your connection to fear. Essentially, you go through the memory of an experience of a traumatic situation so as to be merely watching the event and not re-experiencing it.

Make sure that you're in an environment where you feel safe and secure.

1.   Identify the traumatic or unpleasant memory that you want to diminish.

2.   Remember that you were safe before and after the unpleasant experience.

3.   Imagine yourself sitting in front of your television set and watching yourself on the screen – in black-and-white only.

4.   Now imagine floating out of your chair, out of yourself – and as you float and hover, you can see yourself sitting in your chair and watching the black-and-white film of you on the television screen.

5. Still in black-and-white on the television screen, imagine running the film back to before you experienced the memory you want to diminish and running it through until after the experience when you were safe.

6. Now freeze the film or turn the screen completely white.

7. Now imagine yourself floating into the end of the film.

8. Run the film backwards very quickly – in full color – as if you're experiencing the film, right back to the beginning, when you were safe.

9. Repeat steps 7 and 8 until you're comfortable with the experience.

10. Now go into the future and test yourself against the diminished memory of the once-powerful and fearful memory.

Defining Love For Our Purposes

> *"One word frees us of all the weight and pain of life: That word is love."*

> -   Sophocles

Love refers to a variety of different feelings, states, and attitudes that ranges from interpersonal affection ("I love my mother") to pleasure ("I loved that meal"). It can refer to an emotion of a strong attraction and personal attachment. It can also be a virtue representing human kindness, compassion, and affection – 'the unselfish loyal and benevolent concern for the good of another'. It may also describe compassionate and affectionate actions towards other humans, oneself or animals.

Love may be understood as a function to keep human beings together against menaces and to facilitate the continuation of the species.

There is an old saw that says there is a thin line between love and hate – therefore, love is giving someone the power to destroy you, and trusting them not to.

A dispassionate description of 'love' is the scientific one: Recent studies in neuroscience have indicated that as people fall in love, the brain consistently releases a certain set of chemicals, including the neurotransmitter hormones dopamine, norepinephrine, and serotonin, the same compounds released by amphetamine, stimulating the brain's pleasure center and leading to side effects such as increased heart rate, loss of appetite and sleep, and an intense feeling of excitement. Research has indicated that this stage generally lasts from one and a half to three years.

ENDNOTE: Love can make you do anything and sacrifice for what will be better in the end. Love is intense and passionate. Everything seems brighter, happier and more wonderful when you're in love. If you find it, don't let it go.

Thinking

> *"We can't solve our problems using the same kind of thinking we used when we created them."*

Albert Einstein

This is where you investigate the connection between thinking and feeling, and how you can change the way you feel by changing your thinking.

This is not about trying to better your thinking, or making you a better person. The idea is for you to make changes in your thinking behavior so you can think about yourself exactly how you want to think about yourself.

Usually, we cannot shut off our thinking – we can only think about something else.

In relationships, we can get along if we can find out what we like about others and what we want from the relationship. If we can make some connection – no matter how tenuous – we can use it as a foundation to build on.

Is Dynamic Discovery nonsense because it is just words?

Well, words are all we have that we can rely on, because everything in our life starts with a thought – and our thoughts are only our unspoken words.

All human relationships require communication. When communication ceases, the relationship stops growing and often dies. Words are all we have that we can rely on.

Key Questions

1. What have you been thinking that you don't like? Or what have you been thinking that has not helped you get what you want?

(For a list of unwanted thoughts compiled during actual group sessions, see Page 133)

_____

_____

_____

2. Have you ever thought you were stupid, a failure, etc. after something you've done?

   (Yes) ____   (No) ____

3. If this is what you were thinking, how would you expect to feel?

_____

_____

_____

4. If you were happy, what would you be thinking?

_____

_____

_____

5. What could you do to start thinking that way?

_____

_____

_____

An exercise described in the book shows the connection between the 'feeling' and 'thinking' behaviors. Everyone is asked to close their eyes and do the following, one step at a time, pausing for about 30 seconds to perform each task. To do this exercise on your own, make yourself comfortable and follow the instructions:

1.   Think of the color red.

2.   Think of the color blue.

3.   Think of the color yellow.

4.   Be sad.

5.   Be happy.

6.   Open your eyes and   raise   your right hand.

The object of the exercise is to show you that you can make a conscious decision to change your thoughts and feelings.

Self-evaluate the exercise by asking yourself *"What did I do when I thought of the colors (red, blue, yellow)?"* and *"What did I do to feel happy and sad?"*

How did you do it? Write your answers here:

_____

_____

_____

_____

_____

_____

_____

_____

If you were unable to visualize ('see') the colors or feel the emotions, it's okay – because you will be able to make the exercise work for you by closing your eyes and asking yourself *"What if I could see the colors and feel happy then sad? What would the colors and the emotions 'look' like?"*

Write your answers on the lines above.

The next discussion relates to 'secret' (destructive) thinking, and I recommend that you refer back for this discussion.

NOTE: This session is not about trying to better your thinking. Nor it is about making you a better person. The goal is to make changes in your thinking behavior, so that you can be thinking about yourself in a way that is exactly how you want to think of yourself.

ACTIONS

All behavior is deliberate and purposeful. We choose behaviors in an attempt to meet our needs, or to get what we want. Even if the behavior we choose does not get us what we want, we will continue to choose it until we learn another behavior.

Drinking/drugging is a behavior – a response to a need – that is purposeful and need-fulfilling. Although alcoholism is a disease – it meets the definition of a disease by being chronic, progressive, incurable and potentially fatal – the alcoholic still has the choice over taking the first drink. There can be both an addictive and a behavior component to drinking/drugging, but one can be a heavy user without being an addict. The behavior component is when we use drugs/food/exercise/etc. to avoid, replace, remove or forget our problems.

We cannot have an action without a thought. Our thoughts are often so fast that we are not fully conscious of them – but try to walk or talk or swing your arm without thinking. To hit someone 'without thinking' would seem improbable unless you can makc your arm swing without giving any thought to the action. Try it.

Although there is such a thing as involuntary/reflex actions, they usually occur in bizarre circumstances. Instinct, such as flight and fight, still requires some thoughtful direction, but it may be limited to focusing narrowly on the problem at hand.

Changing what we do is the key to changing how we feel and to getting what we want.

Sometimes we are so caught up in anger, depression or resentment that even changing how we think seems an impossible task. In such situations, a positive change in what we do may be the best we can manage.

Key Questions

1. What have you been doing that you do not like doing? Or that has not helped you get what you want?

(For a list of unwanted actions compiled during actual group sessions, see Page 134.)

_____

_____

_____

_____

_____

2. Which of the actions on the list have you not done?

_____

_____

_____

_____

_____

3. What do you want to be doing?

(For a list of wanted actions compiled during actual group sessions, see Page 134.)

_____

_____

_____

_____

Emotions are a wonderful, immediate and 'alive' source of information about how we are doing and whether we are happy with what is going on in our lives. But it is very, very hard to change our emotions directly. It is easier to change our thinking – to decide, for example, that we will no longer think of ourselves as victims or to decide that in our thoughts, we will concentrate on what we can do rather than what we think everybody else ought to do.

However, there are times that we are so caught up in anger, depression or resentment that even changing how we think seems an impossible task. In such situations, a positive change in what we do may be the best we can manage.

Remember this: Changing what we do is the key to changing how we feel and to getting what we want.

These five questions (and statements) help expedite the self-evaluation process to put you on track to finding better ways to meet your needs:

1. What have you been doing to solve your problem(s)?

_____

_____

_____

2. How is what you are doing helping you get what you want?

It might be helpful to think about your behavior to see how each method is working for you.

_____

_____

_____

3. What might be some other things you could try?

We could look at some new ideas to try when you are ready to look at moving toward a plan.

_____

_____

_____

_____

_____

_____

_____

_____

_____

_____

4. Which idea would you like to try first?

You have several possibilities. Write out what you think about trying any of them.

_____

_____

_____

_____

_____

_____

_____

_____

5. When?

Figure out when to talk about whether your plan is working.

_____

_____

_____

_____

_____

_____

_____

_____

6. Then ask, "What is in it for me? What is in my best interest?"

_____

_____

_____

_____

_____

_____

In psychology, it is assumed that people have certain basic needs – and in Dynamic Discovery, they are classified under five headings for which we apply the acronym LAFFS:

1. **Love and Belonging** – this includes sex, families or loved ones, as well as groups.

2. **Achievement, Power and Recognition** – which includes feeling worthwhile as well as winning.

3. **Freedom** – includes independence, autonomy, your own 'space'.

4. **Fun** – includes pleasure and enjoyment.

5. **Survival** – includes nourishment and shelter.

Whether we are aware of it or not, we are always acting to meet these needs, but we don't necessarily act effectively. Socializing with people is an effective way to meet our need for belonging. Isolating and self-pitying in the hope that people will come to us is generally an ineffective way of meeting that need; it is painful and costly (in psychological terms) and seems to never work in the long-term.

So if life is unsatisfactory, or we are distressed or in trouble, one basic thing to check is whether we are succeeding in meeting the first four of our five basic psychological needs – only those four because the fifth (survival) is implied – because it is in how we meet those four 'psychological' needs that we run into trouble.

The Key Is To Know What We Want

It is not usual to think in terms of meeting our Love and Belonging needs each day as we are more likely to wonder whether a friend would be able to meet us for lunch or to consider getting a group together for a social evening. We may want to meet a friend or mingle with a group or want 'our' football team or 'our' political party to win.

What usually drives us as social beings is our wants, since we don't think of our needs as such. We think of what we want, behave to get what we want, fantasize about what we want and so on. We can check whether we are meeting our wants through addressing three basic questions:

1. What do I want?

_____

_____

_____

_____

2. What am I doing to get what I want?

_____

_____

_____

_____

3. Is it working?

_____

_____

_____

_____

Planning

In order to get what we want, we need to make a plan that is workable – meaning that it is a plan we can successfully implement. In other words, it concentrates on the things that are within our control to do:

- You may not be able to make your spouse talk to you, but you can talk to your spouse.

- You may not be able to make your teenage son treat you with respect, but you can decide that you will no longer provide a laundry and catering service to a son who treats you with contempt.

- You may not be able to make the company give you a promotion, but you can look for a promotion, lobby for it and apply for the job when it comes up.

In answer to the above points and further to the three questions above those points, here are four more questions:

1. Is what I'm doing helping me get what I want? (Yes) ___ (No) ___

2. If not, what might be some other things I could try?

_____

_____

_____

_____

_____

_____

_____

_____

3. Which am I most likely to try first?

_____

_____

_____

4. When will I start?

_____

There are four aspects to everything we do: Thinking, Doing, Feeling and Physiology. So if I am angry, I may think what a rat such-and-such a person is (Thinking), kick the dog (Doing), have that burning angry feeling (Feeling) and have adrenalin and other chemicals in my bloodstream (Physiology). (Again, change the examples to have more effect on the client.)

Take a minute and let that sink in ...

Of these four aspects, the one that is most in our control to change is what we do. Regardless of how we feel, we almost always have some control over what we do.

Law, morality, politeness and many other human institutions recognize this fact. You may feel angry with me but you are not entitled to assault me. You are expected to exercise some control over what you do.

The key point to remember about changing what we do is this:

If you do something that is better than what you are doing now, there is a good chance that your thoughts and feelings will also change in a more positive direction, even though the change may not come straight away.

To put it more simply:

Doing something better than you are doing now will push your feelings towards the positive.

To put it more simply again:

Do better to feel better.

Don't wait until you feel good about doing something that might help. If it might help, do it even though you may not feel enthusiastic at that time.

Doing comes first. First do better; then feel better. In this way, we are empowered by focusing on the power of doing what is within our control to do.

The issue of control is also of great importance.

CONTROL

We are a total behavioral system. The human body is a very smart system that has never been fully duplicated. No other living thing has the power of thought and implementation that a human has, nor the ability for change and correction.

First, there is a thought, which is followed by feelings, actions, and physiological response. The system always behaves. A major elevation in any of the behaviors will generally unbalance the system and take us away from where we really want to go.

As part of meeting our needs, we need control: one person seeks control through position and money; another wants to control his or her physical space, like the teenager who bans all parents and parent-like persons from her room; another wants to chair the committee; another wants an office with a corner and two windows; another wants a specific meal on the table at a specific time.

Control gets us into trouble in two primary ways: when we try to control other people, and when we use drugs and alcohol to give us a false sense of control. At the very heart is the idea that the only person you can really control is yourself. If you think you can control others, you are moving in the direction of frustration. If you think others can control you (and so are to blame for all that goes on in your life), you tend to do nothing and again head for frustration.

There may indeed be things that 'happen' to us and for which we are not personally responsible, but we can choose what we do about these things. Trying to control other people is a losing game; a never-ending battle that alienates us from others and causes endless pain and frustration.

This is why it is vital to stick to what is in our own control to do and to respect the right of other people to meet their needs.

We can, of course, get an instant sense of control from alcohol and some other drugs. Unfortunately, our lives are never more out of control than when we are drunk or drugged. There are very few people in this world who ever woke up with a hangover to find that they had fewer problems than they had when they started using the night before.

Excessive drinking and the use of drugs have to be replaced by doing something else – and that something else has to have a fair chance of getting us what we want in life.

We try to control ourselves, people and situations to meet our needs or to get what we want.

Often we are not aware that we are doing this. We may walk to the shop to buy something we want but be unaware of our surroundings as we walk down the street. Indeed, we may be 'a million miles away' in our minds, daydreaming about something but still end up in the shop we wanted to go to; we were able to control our direction and our walking even though we were not aware of what we were doing!

Everybody needs a certain amount of control to meet their needs for power, belonging, freedom and fun. The most important word to notice here is 'everybody'.

You need a certain amount of control. Your partner needs a certain amount of control. The boss needs a certain amount of control, but so does the worker. The parent needs a certain amount of control, but so does the child. The customer needs a certain amount of control, but so does the shopkeeper.

When people fail to recognize that the other person also has a need for control, the stage is set for conflict. If, however, we are willing to negotiate and compromise, we can find ways to co-operate and create a better life.

Sometimes we ask for what we want. This respects the sense of control of both parties. (If you don't believe asking is an attempt to gain some control, consider the outrage in the workhouse when Oliver Twist asked for more.) Sometimes instead of asking, we demand what we want. But demanding what we want ignores the other person's sense of control – and they will want to resist us.

Control is all around you. For example:

- If you're scared to go to work and stay in bed instead, you're controlling your situation at least to the extent of not going to work.

- If you buy a lottery ticket, you are trying to exercise a little bit of control over your future, however poor the chances of winning.

- If you hear there's going to be a gasoline shortage and you hoard gasoline, you're trying to gain a little control over the future.

- If you boss people around, you are trying to get control over them.

- And if they find a way to cheat you or con you, they are trying to get some of their control back.

Key Concepts Of Control:

1. All we ever do is behave (good or bad).

2. We are externally motivated by the world around us.

3. If we are sad, unhappy or depressed, it is because we choose to feel and behave that way.

4. We are not victims of our past unless we choose to be.

5. We are constantly seeking to live in our 'ideal' world.

The ideal world is your personal Shangri-La – the ideal of what you want your life to be. It fulfills your most basic needs by placing the actual people you want to love in your ideal world. If you have no one in your ideal world or are experiencing conflict between your ideal world and their 'real' world, there is an approach for that – if you can accept that there is not one 'right' way to view things. Different views may be just as valid and may fit the facts just as well. Views that keep you stuck are simply not useful.

Sometimes all that is necessary to initiate significant change is a shift in your perception of the situation (which is the value of a group setting – more and different perspectives).

Focus on what is possible and changeable rather than what is impossible and intractable. Focus on aspects of your situation that seem most changeable.

• To create a solution to your problem, it is best if you can believe that you do not have to analyze a problem in order to solve it. Indeed, focusing on the problem may actually be unhelpful because your focus can become an obsession from which you cannot divert your attention (the elephant in the living room).

• Start from a premise that you have all the strengths and qualities you need to solve your difficulties – it is simply a question of effectively mobilizing them.

If we control acting and thinking, then feeling and physiology will follow. We choose our behaviors. The only behavior an individual can control is his or her own.

Control Car

We are a total behavioral system. No other living thing has the power of thought and implementation that a human has, nor the ability for change and correction.

First, there is a thought – which is followed by feelings, actions, and physiological response. The system always behaves. A major elevation in any of the behaviors will generally unbalance the system and take us away from where we really want to go.

The human body is a smart system that's never been fully duplicated in nature. No other living thing has the power of thought and implementation that a human has, nor the ability for change or correction. A front-wheel drive car, like the one pictured below, with well-balanced 'tires', will drive us properly in the direction we want to go. First there's a thought which is followed by feelings, actions and physiological response.

Balanced Example

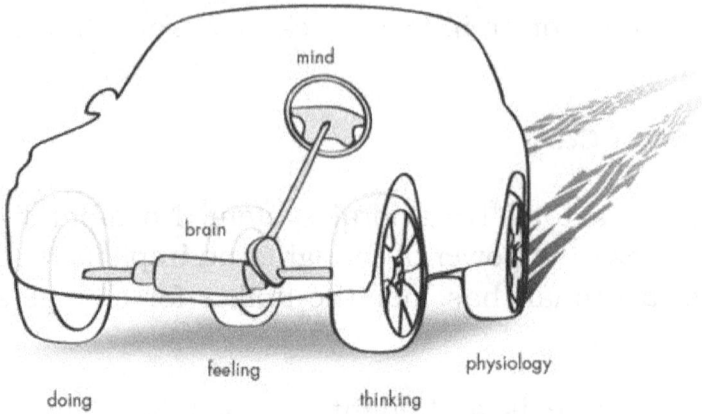

Any major elevation in one or more of our Behaviors would have the same effect as greatly over-inflating a particular tire. Similarly, repression of our Behaviors has the same effect as deflating a particular tire. Either way, it'll cause us to feel 'unbalanced'.

An Unbalanced Example (shown below)

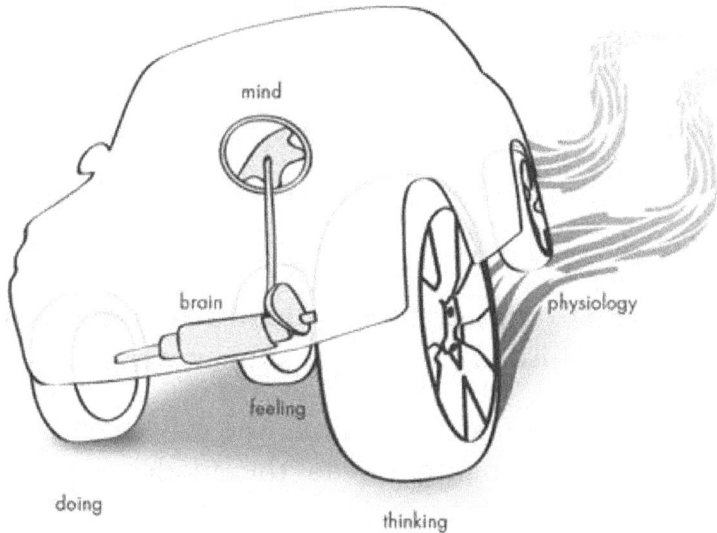

In the example shown above, the thinking 'tire' is obsessive (greatly inflated), the feelings are 'somewhat' inflated, and the actions are 'somewhat' deflated (becomes less active). Done long enough and your health (physiology) could suffer. This car would not steer well – it would not be taking you in the direction you want to go.

Control Computer

The way to change how we feel and what we do is to change our thinking with a new program. The old program and everything we ever learned will always be with us, but we can access the new program and evaluate it for applicability in whatever situation we are in. If we think that the old ways had some value, we can always call them up and evaluate how they actually worked by applying our memory/conscience – or by implementing the actual behavior again.

Using the computer analogy allows us to slow our response time and fully evaluate a behavior prior to implementation.

Theory

The Control Computer theory illustrates how we can change our thinking to change our lives.

Computer manufacturers mimic the way the human mind works by using us as the model for their products. The human mind is very smart, and the way computers query and sort information somewhat mirrors the human ability for change and correction. The way to change how we think is by trying out a new 'program'.

Since all change is stressful, it is comforting to know that the old program will always be in our memory (or hard drive) allowing us the choice between old and new Behaviors (or programs). If, at any time we want to revisit our old Behaviors we just have to access our memory and take a look. In addition, if the new Behaviors are too extreme we can replace them with another new program – totally new or a blend of our old Behavior and the new.

Computer

In the illustration below, the keyboard represents our thoughts and the monitor represents our mind which forms judgments. A computer's 'judgments' are saved in the memory of one or more drives, while ours are saved in our minds' memory. By hitting 'Print', the computer performs an action attached to the thought.

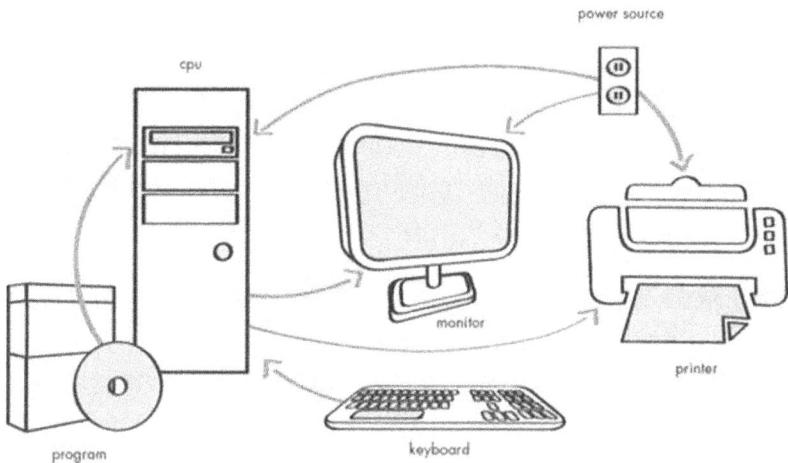

The major difference between the human mind and a computer is that the human mind has the ability to create concepts, whereas a computer can only deal with information that it has.

Let that sink in ...

If we think about a problem that has no readily available answer because we haven't experienced it before, our human mind will come up with outlandish and crazy search results we have no business paying attention to.

A computer can be programmed to make projections, but it does not spontaneously create concepts. To your mind, perception is reality. In many instances, if your mind can conceive it, your body will follow.

The function of the conscious mind is to take in information. The subconscious mind takes responsibility for filing and retrieving that information, and for weighing it against your Values and Beliefs systems. The new information is strengthened or diluted depending on whether it matches your Values and Beliefs systems.

The subconscious mind exists to serve us and will try to find a way for us to get what we want – sometimes to our own detriment. For example:

A person sits on the edge of their bed, ready for sleep, and thinks, "Well, I suppose I'll toss and turn all night, and not get any sleep." Their subconscious will do everything it can to oblige them by interrupting their sleep.

Or prior to going to sleep, they consider some unpleasant things they're scheduled to do the next day. They think, "Man, tomorrow will probably be a really terrible day." Their subconscious will do everything it can to oblige them by putting them in a sour mood.

A computer, when asked to find information that it doesn't have, will search its files and then provide a message advising that the information was not found, and asking whether you want it to continue searching. We must then select one of two options – 'Continue searching' or 'Cancel'.

The human mind, on the other hand – when asked to find information that it does not have – will search and search and search to no end. It does not provide a message asking whether you want it to continue or cancel, and its ability to create concepts can provide some very interesting results. For example:

A person is seriously troubled by a financial problem, and they have no training or experience in solving this type of problem. Their mind will search for solutions that do not exist. They're obsessed – because this problem really offends their Values and Beliefs – so they think and think, and think. At some point, they may ask themselves, "What's going to happen if I can't solve this serious financial problem?" Their mind might take this as an instruction to create a concept, and the concept may create a picture of the person ending up living on the street and eating out of garbage bins – their life ruined, a disgrace. If that's not bad enough, their body will react to that concept, or perception, as though it was real.

A person has been threatened with extreme physical violence by someone they're afraid of. They have no experience in dealing with a situation like this. They think and think about what to do, and no answer appears. Their mind creates a concept whereby every noise in the house represents someone breaking in, and they see an intruder in every shadow. At some point, the stress will drive them into total collapse – even if the threat was never, ever, actually carried out.

A person who is afraid of the dark is locked in a room with no light source. Within a period of time, they will begin to imagine terrifying presences. Although in reality, nothing is there – their bodies react as though the concept is real.

Let that sink in ...

To the human mind, perception is reality. In many instances, if our mind can conceive it, our mind and body can achieve it – regardless of whether the concept is helpful or hurtful.

The subconscious part of your mind is the storage area which holds all of the information that you've accumulated throughout your lifetime – every experience, everything you've seen, heard, felt, smelled, touched and experienced. And it's all filed away as message units sorted into message clusters, or topics.

If you were a computer, your subconscious mind would be the hard drive. Your conscious mind would be the RAM (random access memory), and your Values and Beliefs systems would be the program.

The major difference between the human mind and a computer is that the human mind has the ability to create concepts, whereas a computer can only deal with information it has within its programs.

Physiology And Total Behavior

At any time, four things are happening for us: what we are doing, what we are thinking, what we are feeling, and what is going on in our bodies – and sometimes these activities work in harmony. For instance, if we are pleased, we may be smiling (doing), thinking positive thoughts, feeling content and physically relaxed. If we are angry, we may be shouting (doing), thinking angry thoughts, feeling that we are in a rage, and having our hearts beat quickly and our muscles tensed up.

Often, the four activities are going in different directions. If you are sitting in a dentist's waiting room and you hear the drill starting up, your feelings may tell you to run but your thinking may tell you to stay. Your body may be tensed up with heart racing and adrenaline pumping. And what you are doing may be thumbing idly through an out-of-date copy of Time magazine... and appearing calm, cool and collected.

You could say that at any one time, we are behaving in each of these four ways: feeling, thinking, doing, physiology. We can call this combination our Total Behavior. If we can change one of these, then we have a good chance of changing the others.

It is hard to change our feelings directly. It is easier to change what we are thinking, and easiest of all to change what we are doing.

So the golden rule is: if you want to change how you feel, begin by changing what you are doing or what you are thinking. Easy to say and hard to do? Yes! Let's look at it a little more closely by briefly reviewing what we have already learned.

Change

Although the four components of Behavior are Doing, Thinking, Feeling, and Physiology, it is best if you are purpose-led instead of feelings-led. You are still very aware of your feelings – they are the warm, beating heart of your life – but your purpose is your moment-to-moment guide and your orientation is towards thinking and doing.

By focusing on what you can do rather than on what you feel, you arrive at a point where your feelings become pleasant and positive – but sometimes you cannot move ahead unless you change what you want.

Let that sink in ...

In order to bring about change in your life, you must do something different or change what you want – and that involves a change in thinking or doing. However, if your emotions are running wild – with grief or depression, for instance – it would not be unusual that all you can change is what you do ...

and then your thoughts, like your feelings and physiology, have to follow.

Key Questions

1. In what ways have activities that you haven't liked doing affected your physiology?

_____

_____

_____

_____

_____

_____

_____

2. How would your life look if things were the way you wanted?

_____

_____

_____

_____

_____

3. What is something you can do to help you get what you want?

BEHAVIOR AND RELATIONSHIPS

The surest way to bring people into your circle (closer to you) may be to attract them in through behavior changes.

If Self = Best Interest, then who is the best person to look after your best interest?

For Dynamic Discovery purposes, best interest is defined as not being deliberately hurtful or harmful to self or others.

> You operate as a 'smart system' that is capable of evaluating for your needs and determining what to do in order to meet those needs. Once you build your library of activities and events that will help you meet your needs, your 'smart system' will evaluate and choose the best option(s).
>
> Because no other person can live your life for you, it follows that you are the one person on this planet who can restore your own dignity and self-respect. No one else can do that for you.

Key Questions

1. How has your behavior affected your relationships?

_____

_____

_____

_____

_____

_____

2. What are your best interests, and where are you in relation to them?

_____

_____

_____

_____

_____

_____

Activities

1. Diagram your relationships as affected by your behavior.   (relationship circles)

This is an example of one client's 'Ideal World':

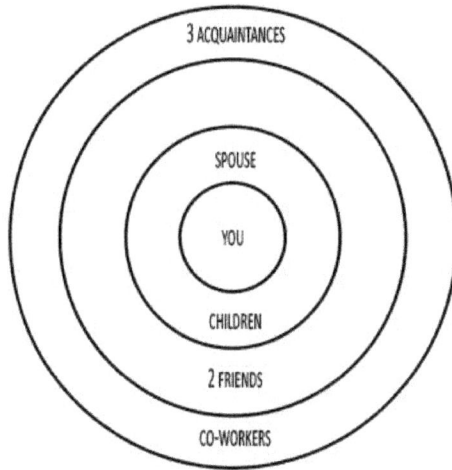

The chart below is for you to use to show how your relationships actually are:

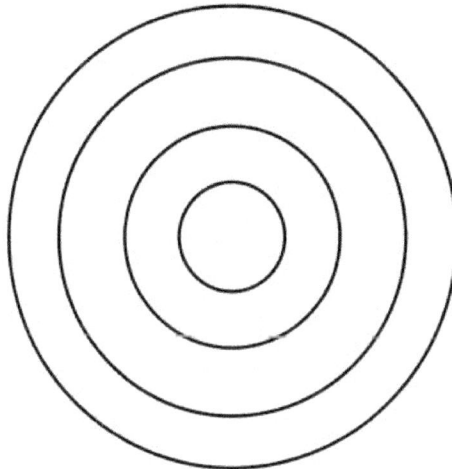

2.　Self-evaluate the relationship between your current behavior and your best interests.

_____

_____

_____

_____

_____

_____

_____

_____

_____

_____

_____

_____

NEEDS AND RELATIONSHIPS

Although we always strive to meet our five basic needs (LAFFS), in Dynamic Discovery we only evaluate for the first three needs:

1. Love and Belonging

2. Achievement, Power and Recognition

3. Freedom

The fourth need is Fun, which is generally met when the three primary needs are in balance.

The fifth need is Survival, and by merely showing up, you acknowledge that.

When self-evaluating the ways that you use to meet your needs, you can determine whether it is the activity or the people, or both, that is need-fulfilling.

You can use an activity or relationship to meet more than one need, and you can evaluate how to meet your needs to a greater extent. That puts you in control of how much quality you have in your life and how to get it.

When a relationship fails to meet your needs, you may find upon evaluation that a selection error has occurred or that the relationship never met one of your basic needs – maybe it was a relationship based upon guilt or dependency or enabling, rather than being based upon a 'need' connection.

Key Questions

1. What do you think you have been doing to get your needs met?

_____

_____

_____

_____

2. What needs are being met by your relationships?

_____

_____

_____

_____

3. What could you do instead to meet your needs?

_____

_____

_____

_____

Activities

1. Draw out your Needs Circle to chart behaviors and relationships which satisfy your basic needs. The chart below is from one client's 'Ideal World'. The figure below can be used to draw your actual Needs chart.

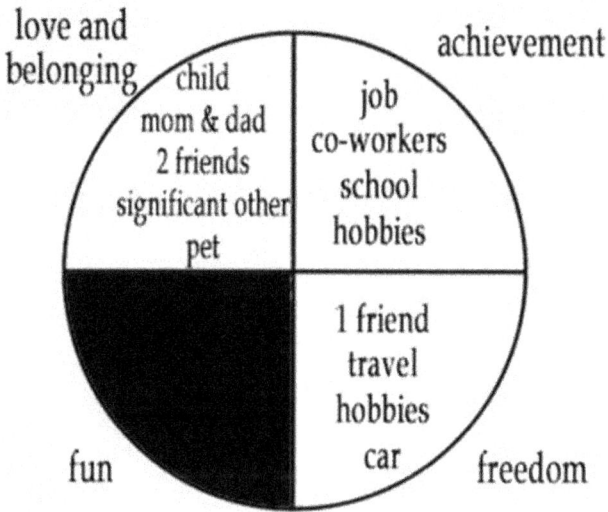

love and
belonging   achievement

child
mom & dad
2 friends
significant other
pet

job
co-workers
school
hobbies

1 friend
travel
hobbies
car

fun   freedom

2. Write out ways for you to start to satisfy your unmet needs.

_____

_____

_____

_____

_____

_____

_____

_____

_____

_____

_____

_____

_____

_____

FUTURIZE YOUR FANTASY

(Having your world the way you want it to be)

Purpose: To identify the needs you are controlling for. This exercise is not designed to resolve issues – it is designed to start meeting needs.

Plan:

1. If your world was the way you wanted it five years from now, what would it 'look' like? (Thinking, Doing, Feeling)

2. Writing it out is more effective and hooks into our beliefs.

Criteria:

1. Not dependent on anyone else to make it happen.

2. Occurs five years in the future.

3. Takes place on this planet.

4. For general audiences only (not sexually explicit).

The purpose is to identify what needs we are controlling for.

Evaluation:

1. Look for the energy and the needs being met by your fantasy.

2. The fantasy is a way to get permission to enter the new world being envisioned.

3. What would you be thinking, doing and feeling if your world was exactly the way you wanted it to be?

So how do you work out your fantasy? In an actual Dynamic Discovery workshop, the leader provides a scenario and asks the group some questions:

You go to sleep tonight and something magical happens. All the desired advances in your life have taken place. The magical event happens while you are asleep so you don't actually know that it has happened.

When you wake up in the morning, what is the first thing that you will notice you are doing that will tell you the magical event has happened?

What next?

Each person writes words or draws a picture or series of pictures to represent the differences in their actions. This becomes their Futurized Fantasy.

Now write out your response to the scenario and the questions:

dynamic discovery
a process of self-evaluation

1. When you wake up in the morning, what is the first thing that you will notice you are doing that will tell you the magical event has happened?

_____

_____

_____

2. What next?

_____

_____

_____

3. Write words or draw a picture or series of pictures to represent the differences in your actions.

_____

_____

_____

_____

_____

_____

DARN GOOD START

This is where we get to start working out solutions and finding ways to start experiencing some victories, and to start building more quality into our lives. Remember, we do not evaluate for right and wrong, or for good and bad. What is is. What ain't ain't. You can't be measured by someone else's yardstick.

Criteria:

1. Must be easy to do and not doing now.

2. Must be something we want to do.

3. Must be tangible, reportable and timely (doable within 48 to 72 hrs).

4. Doing it once is rewarding.

5. Continuing to do Darn Good Starts (DGSs) will help meet the need.

6. It must address the need rather than the want.

This is our prescription for meaningful change. Continuous and constant application conditions us to structure winning and control in our lives. We always use LAFFS to determine what we are DGSing for:

dynamic discovery

1. Are you interested in finding something else to do that will get you what you really want?

(Yes) ___   (No) ___

If you don't know, do a fantasy exercise to find the need(s) you want to satisfy.

2. The action might involve just making a list of things we might like to do and aren't doing now.

3. Define your expectation of a DGS, and what a DGS would look like to you. One way is to ask yourself, "What would I want to be doing if I knew I could not fail?"

_____

_____

_____

4. You must understand and deal with the way things really are.

5. Is it safe? (Yes) ___   (No) ___

Write out your DGS below.

_____

_____

_____

_____

_____

_____

_____

_____

_____

_____

_____

_____

_____

_____

SOLUTIONS

Key Questions

1. Are you interested in finding something else to do that will get you what you really want?

(Yes) ____   (No) ____

If your answer was yes, describe what that 'something else' is:

_____

_____

_____

2. Is it easily attainable?   (Yes) ____   (No) ____

If your answer was yes, describe how you plan to attain it:

_____

_____

_____

_____

3. Is it an action that is reportable?

(Yes) ____   (No) ____

Indicate to whom you will report:

_____

_____

4. Is it something you want to do?

(Yes) ____   (No) ____

Describe why you want to do it:

_____

_____

_____

5. Will you benefit by doing it once?

(Yes) ____   (No) ____

Describe what benefits you 'see':

_____

_____

6. If you keep doing it, will it meet your needs?

(Yes) ____   (No) ____

Describe how you 'see' it meeting your needs:

_____

_____

_____

Activities

1. Evaluate your written fantasy for evidence of unmet needs.

Describe how you 'see' your unmet needs:

_____

_____

_____

_____

_____

_____

2. Planning win-win solutions.

Describe in detail what would constitute a solution – describe it as you 'see' it:

_____

_____

_____

_____

_____

_____

_____

Because I've used the 'magic' question (involving a sudden miraculous solution) in several places within this workbook, I want to explain the reason: We use it because we want people to feel the answer, to experience it, and not just to think about it. This helps to make the imagined future more real and not just a theoretical construct.

Visualizing is a way to get you to 'go inside' for a few moments and really 'see and feel' the question.

With your eyes closed, imagine the following: If, by some very real magic, you were to go to sleep tonight and a miracle happened while you were sleeping, and when you woke in the morning, you and your life was in an altogether happier place, as if the problem has been swept away... just imagine how that would feel. How will it be? What will you do?

Take some time to carry out this visualization exercise and then write out the answers to the following questions:

Describe how it felt:

_____

Describe how it will be:

_____

_____

_____

Describe what you will do:

_____

_____

_____

This exercise will:

- give you a flavour and a 'blueprint' for how things might be different

- give you an idea of how to manage your expectations and develop a strategy for future work.

Sometimes people need a little coaxing to enter into the spirit of 'fantasy' questioning. And sometimes we all need encouragement to see the good things that have already occurred or are happening right now. Using this type of question is a wonderful way to bypass the usual worries about how things could change, and to switch to a motivational focus on what you really want changed.

In hypnotherapy, we use a variation of this approach by first inducing a full state of relaxation, which diverts the client's focus away from the problem. Some 50 years ago, Milton Erickson (a well-regarded psychiatrist and hypnotherapist) presented the original version of the 'magic' question which involved asking his client to look into the future and see themselves as they wanted to be, with problems solved, and then to explain what had happened to cause this change to come about. He sometimes also asked clients to think of a date in the future, then worked backwards, asking them what had happened at various points on the way.

Since Erickson's time, thousands of counselors and therapists have adopted and/or adapted the magic question and used it to take the pressure off their clients so as to allow them to 'freewheel' their imagination and describe what they were really missing in their lives.

Personally, I propose it as a very specific question: "Suppose that while you are relaxing, a magical event has occurred and the problem that brought you here is solved. However, because you are so relaxed, you don't know that the magical event has already happened. When you return to full awareness, you will notice that some things will be different and those things will make you aware that the magical event has taken place. Before you leave my office, you will be able to begin to tell me what is different about you and your life."

AFTERWORD

Thank you for your interest in Dynamic Discovery.

We would love to hear from you. You can connect with us through our website, www.dynamicdiscovery.ca.

Here are a couple of things for you to remember:

- Whenever I am distressed by external things, I have found that my distress is due to my perception of the thing and not to the thing itself. Through the Dynamic Discovery process, I now know how to suspend my perception so as to properly assess whether the distress is real or imagined.

- Once you adopt an attitude of gratitude, you will soon feel truly secure in yourself – it is then that you can really start experiencing the kind of life you desire.

- Nothing is particularly hard if you are able to divide it into small jobs.

It is important for you to understand that your background is an extremely important part of who you are, but it isn't cast in concrete. You can get over it. It's never too late to have a happy childhood. Every day you have new experiences which tomorrow will be part of your background.

Too many people carry their background around with them as if it's a burden that is keeping them from living the rest of their lives – instead of treating it as a learning experience. You can even break patterns that have gone on for generations.

You have to conquer the demons inside you. Otherwise you will pass them on to your children. The demons are your fearful memories; you have to face them and defeat your fears. All courage and strength must be developed by facing our fearful memories and then transcending them by creating a stronger memory.

Sometimes people use age as a convenient excuse to avoid improving their lives: "I'm too old to start something new", or, "I couldn't learn that at my age". Other people, though, go on to achieve their greatest accomplishments in life in later years.

It's not important how old you are; what is important is how you think, how you feel, and what you do. Feelings lead to attitudes, attitudes become beliefs, and beliefs become the basis for actions – no matter what your age. Thoughts lead to purposes; purposes go forth in action; actions form habits; habits decide character; and character fixes our destiny. Just adjust your thinking and your age will keep pace.

What if all your problems are just memories?

Think of a problem that you used to believe you had. If you are having a hard time accepting that the

126

problem is behind you, include every moment that has passed as part of the past. Think of the past as anything that is not happening right now and you can see what choices are available to you with clearer eyes.

Because this is a big change in our thinking, it requires conscious effort to make it a familiar response. Repetition is how we learn. If we're no longer tied to the mistakes of our past, we're free to make decisions based on reason and we'll always be centered enough to respond rather than react. This approach teaches us to remember how we used to behave in a certain way, so that we can finally let go of behaving that way out of habit.

It may sound bizarre, but it works. And it's enlightening. So many of the things we used to believe about ourselves don't have to hold true anymore – not if we don't want them to. So that voice in your head that used to say, "I always pick the wrong direction," or "I'm always late for important stuff," doesn't need to be true right now. That can be the old story.

That was then, this is now; that's the root of this new way of thinking that challenges us to take responsibility by seeing that we actually create our problems by expecting them. If we believe that we have a problem, then we focus on whatever validates that belief.

I have personally found that my life is much, much better and I am much happier when I am grateful –

when I develop an attitude of gratitude. In fact, it's one of the most powerful feelings I have ever had.

However, I'm not grateful for the things I own, like my car or my clothing. I'm not grateful for my toys. I do, for the most part, enjoy them, but I'm not grateful for them – because in a flash, they could be taken away... just like all the people who have lost all their possessions (and friends and family) in tragedies like natural disasters or by the acts of people filled with hatred and rage.

For my happiness to be attached to possessions sets me up to be unhappy way too easily. An attitude of gratitude is why many people who have experienced great setbacks have been able to quickly turn in the right direction and start again, just as determined and certain of success as before... because they are grateful for what they DO have.

As for me, what I am grateful for is the knowledge, ability and willingness to learn even more. I am also thankful for the opportunities to use my knowledge and experience so that I can give what I have learned to others.

In addition, I am thankful for my past and current challenges, which have taught and will continue to teach me and strengthen me so that I can overcome and triumph over adversity in the future.

You see, it is these things for which I AM grateful that make everything else in my life work. If I lose my possessions, I can get them all back and more because I have an attitude of gratitude ... at least I have it most of the time.

And what I am most grateful for is the love I share with those close to me and the regard and acceptance I share and receive from people in all walks of life whom I meet socially and through work – many of whom have become friends.

When a person thinks about the people, things, and experiences that they're grateful for, their awareness of the good in their life increases and they start to feel good. What you focus on increases and you have even more to be grateful for.

If enough of us can be gratefully aware of the ways in which we can help each other in times of trouble, more and more people will be helped to work through the inevitable stressful hazards that confront us all.

It is remarkable to see the power that ordinary people have to adapt to reality, however unpleasant. They have a great deal more strength than we often give them credit for. Unassisted in a time of crisis, this strength may fail them – but if we recognize it and build it up, we can help each other through times of trouble.

Ask yourself: is what you're practicing today about where you've been, or where you want to be? Practice feeling how you'll feel and practice doing what you'll do when you get where you're going. Today is practice for tomorrow.

If you really like adventures, here's an interesting affirmation to try on for size: "I am willing that my present and future be totally unlike my past." Willingness is the key.

Finally, consider this: You are the spearhead of evolution. Think about it – you've survived for long enough on this planet to be reading this piece, which means you are extraordinarily super. In fact, you come from a long line of ancestors who managed to survive and have kids, too! All the lessons of those countless years of evolution have been encoded in your brilliant neurology.

You are so much more than you think you are, so you can allow your idea of yourself to begin to open up. You might even become curious about just how much more is possible for you than you previously thought. How much more love, joy, happiness, freedom, fulfillment, leisure time, fun and adventure is possible?

Fill your boots! You are the spearhead of evolution.

REMEMBER THIS...

For those of you who are really 'stuck' because of your 'limiting' Values and Beliefs, you will find a free downloadable workbook (What Are Your Values?) on our website (www.DynamicDiscovery.ca) that was specially devised to provide a concise, systematic way to change those Values and Beliefs that are interfering with your ability to be happy.

TYPICAL WORDS FOR THE EXERCISES

(Recorded from actual group sessions)

Have You Ever Had A Feeling You Didn't Like? (at any time in your life)

Anger	Anxious	Apart from
Dependent	Depressed	Different
Discontent	Failure	Frustrated
FEAR (a distressing emotion aroused by impending danger, evil or pain.)		
Hate	Hopeless	Impotent
Inadequate	Incapable	Incompetent
Incomplete	Isolated	Insulted
Lonely	Not desired	Numb
Out of control	Pain	Revengeful
Sad	Separated	Slighted
Spiteful	Tense	Ugly
Unattractive	Uncomfortable	Unhealthy
Unimportant	Unloved	Unhappy
Uninteresting		Unintelligent (stupid) Different
Uninvolved	Unsuccessful	Unvalued
Unwanted	Useless	Weak

What Would You Sooner Be Feeling?

Accessible	Adequate	Attractive
Calm	Capable	Comfortable
Complete	Content	Desired
Handsome	Happy	Healthy
Honest	Important	In control
Independent	Involved	Intelligent (smart)
Interested (ing)	Loved (ing)	Part of
Peaceful	Powerful	Respected
Sexy	Strong	Successful
Valued	Wanted	

Have You Ever Had A Thought You Didn't Like? (at any time in your life)

Confused

Hidden Rules   (What were the do's and don'ts ?)

   - shoulds/shouldn'ts

   - can't do

   - could have done

   - musts/must nots

Nicknames   (What did you call yourself?)

Spin dryer

How Would You Sooner Be Thinking?

Calm	Compassionate	Dependable
Fun	Kind	Loving
Strong		

Have You Ever Done Something You Didn't Like? (at any time in your life)

Abuse	Arguing	Blaming
Cheating	Crying	Depressing
Drinking	Drugging	Gossiping
Lying	Spying	Revenging
Self-Pitying	Sexing	Shout
Sicking	Swearing	Violence
Yelling		

What Would You Sooner Be Doing?

Accepting	Assertive	Attractive
Caring	Compassionate	Confident
Courageous	Exercising	Honest
Loving	Open-minded	Peaceful
Sharing	Smart	Spiritual
Strong	Trusting	Volunteering

TYPICAL QUESTIONS FOR THE EXERCISES

Introductions

1. What has been going on that led you here?

2. What have you done to try to resolve your problems?

3. How did it work out? Did it help you get what you want?

4. What do you want?

5. If you got that, what would it mean to you?

Feelings

6. What feelings have you had in your life that you didn't like?

7. How many hours a day are you dealing with feelings you don't like?

8. Which of the feelings on our list have you not felt?

9. Are your feelings the biggest problem you have?

10. How would you like to be feeling?

Thinking

11. What have you been thinking that you don't like? Or, has not helped you get what you want?

12. Have you ever thought you were stupid, a failure, etc., after something you've done?

13. If this is what you are thinking, how would you expect to feel?

14. If you were happy, what would you be thinking?

15. What could you do to start thinking that way?

Doing (Actions)

16. What have you been doing that you do not like doing? Or has not helped you get what you want?

17. Which of the actions on the list have you not done?

18. What do you want to be doing?

Physiology

19. In what ways have activities that you haven't liked doing affected your physiology?

20. How would your life look if things were the way you wanted?

21. What is something you can do to help you get what you want?

Behavior And Relationships

22. How has your behavior affected your relationships?

23. What are your best interests, and where are you in relation to them?

Needs Circles

24. What do you think you have been doing to get your needs met?

25. What needs are being met by your relationships?

26. What could you do instead to meet your needs?

Solutions (win-win)

27. Are you interested in finding something else to do that will get you what you really want?

28. Is it easily attainable?

29. Is it an action that is reportable?

30. Is it something you want to do?

31. Will you benefit by doing it once?

32. If you keep doing it, will it meet your needs?